10 Leadership Contracts

Key Strategies to Build POWER Teams:
Passion . Ownership . Wellness
Excellence . Relationships

Dr. Joe Currier

First Edition – September 2012

ISBN
978-1-4602-0299-9 (Hardcover)
978-1-4602-0298-2 (Paperback)
978-1-4602-0300-2 (eBook)

I have gone to great lengths to protect the privacy of my clients. I have permission to share their stories, but changed their names and any other identifying markers. Their stories are accurate, but their data points are altered.

Published by:

FriesenPress
Suite 300 – 852 Fort Street
Victoria, BC, Canada V8W 1H8

www.friesenpress.com

Distributed to the trade by The Ingram Book Company

THIS BOOK IS DEDICATED TO THE MEN AND WOMEN OF THE ALLEGIS GROUP

who continue to serve the vision and mission of Stephen Bisciotti, Jim Davis, Michael Salandra, John Carey, Tom Thornton, and the first generation of leaders:

Strive for Excellence Through Serving Others

A SPECIAL THANK YOU TO

Todd Mohr, President of Aerotek
Jay Alvather, President of TEK Systems
Simon Robinson, President of Major, Lindsey & Africa

You inspire the people you serve through your dedication to excellence without forgetting that the greatness of any organization is its people.

10 LEADERSHIP CONTRACTS

To Build POWER Teams

*

Passion . **O**wnership . **W**ellness . **E**xcellence . **R**elationships

Members of *POWER*[*] teams make
dollars and cents by making
dollar and sense—common sense!

HOW? By first building leadership contracts that reflect the values, passions, needs and expectations of each **partner**.

Not employees or coworkers...
PARTNERS!

POWER

Passion . **O**wnership . **W**ellness . **E**xcellence . **R**elationships

For more information regarding the concept of "POWER TEAMS", please see SIDEBAR REGARDING *P.O.W.E.R. PERFORMANCE*: Page 58.

Business results that consistently exceed the norm—repeatable championship level performances—are driven by passionate individuals who share a bond based upon trust, respect, clearly defined expectations, accountability, and recognition and rewards for excellence.

POWER-TEAMS **ARE RARE**

Many people in the workplace believe that they are part of a "team." In my opinion, in most instances, they are wrong. At best, the overwhelming majority of businessmen and –women are members of efficient and effective **groups**.

And while that is not a bad thing, it is also not something that will distinguish individuals as exceptional or create the levels of reward and satisfaction that can be attained if they were members of a dynamic team.

The primary differences in attitude and behavior of members of power-**teams** versus efficient-effective **groups** are summarized in Table 1 (at the end of this chapter).

Various forces unite members of a team when they form specific *contracts*. Some articles of these *contracts* are explicit. Others are implied. All are important in order to produce the passion and discipline needed to excite, unite and drive individuals toward a common goal.

Members of efficient and effective **groups** tend to remain relatively narrowly focused, utilizing fundamental business KSA's (Knowledge-Skills-Abilities)

* POWER is an acronym to define very unique teams that build their performance and legacy through five forces

to gain negotiated material rewards for their work. To them, business is just a job that rewards people when they succeed and holds them accountable when they underachieve. If someone within the group gets too personal and attempts to penetrate the *privacy barrier*, they inquire, *"What does that have to do with business."*

Members of power-**teams**, on the contrary, know that business is both a job AND a life-adventure. While material rewards and career opportunities are important, these business incentives are the outcome, not the underlying driving force behind hard work. Don't get me wrong, power-team (P-T) partners may be organizational patriots inspired by a common cause, but they are not "corporate monks," who dismiss wealth and traditional success markers like job-opportunity, position-power and the finer things of life. However, these factors are the fruits of one's labor, not the primary motivation.

The unique qualities of a *PT* are represented in Table 1. Not in one column versus the other. The real strength is represented by the power of AND, not an either-or equation. That is to say, *PT* partners manage the traditional business forces in the left column such as the supervisory prerogatives of the "boss" and non-negotiable responsibilities arising from performance contracts. They accept these fiscal and supervisory realities of corporate life AND respond passionately to opportunities that occur on the right side of the chart by forming special bonds with men and women who are driven by a desire to compete to win! Members of *power-teams* form contracts that bind individuals in a unique adventure—one that leaves a legacy that makes dollars and **cents** and dollars and **sense**—common sense.

Table 1. Efficient–Effective GROUP

1. Businessmen and -women who are driven primarily by bottom-line results and material reward. . . Business Mercenaries
2. Performance contracts that manage employee behavior through control and intimidation.
3. Independent performance is the norm. Self-centered competition—even when counter-productive to the team's overall mission—is tolerated, rewarded, and even modeled.
4. Employees are accountable to senior managers often through overt or implied fear for one's job. Coaching is a supervisor's responsibility.
5. Leadership is the responsibility of the highest ranking associate.
6. Employees operate in an environment of minimal levels of safety and trust. People expect personal privacy and generally separate their lives from their work.
7. Inconsistent use of cultural norms that tolerate or even reward "at risk achievement"–that is, performance that produces financial profit in the absence of core values and character-based behavior.
8. Ambiguous, contradictory and inconsistent rules of engagement and interpersonal conflict. Gossip, rumors, and destructive confrontation are common.

Table 1A. POWER TEAM

1. Businessmen and -women motivated by a shared vision that strikes an emotional chord... Organizational Patriots
2. Shared performance goals that spark pride, passion and a spirit to compete to win.
3. Independent initiative balanced by collegial shared-work-product promote healthy competition. A spirit of self-responsibility and personal achievement are aligned with inter-dependent efforts to attain the team's overall mission.
4. Partners are primarily accountable to self ("Am I giving it my all?") and to job partners. Peer-coaching and sharing best practices are expected and rewarded.
5. Leadership is the responsibility of every partner who can add value to a situation.
6. Deeper level of trust and respect—vulnerability-based trust. Individuals build relationships by prudently sharing their life-stories—how significant life-events have impacted them positively and negatively. Partners recognize the fact that "Human behavior determines business behavior."
7. "Success" is defined both quantitatively (profit) and qualitatively (relationships, character, satisfaction). Power-performers meet benchmark performance standards while reflecting the organization's values and cultural norms.
8. Clear and consistent rules of engagement grounded in healthy tension and "care-frontation" in the spirit of the "Team Rule" (described in the 3rd Contract) are utilized to build productive and satisfying competitive partnerships.

10 LEADERSHIP CONTRACTS

To Build POWER **Teams**

According to the dictionary, a contract is a formal agreement or the writing containing it. A contract, whether stated or implied, is an arrangement, a compact, covenant, or deal.

To members of a power-performance team, a contract is more. It is a **PROMISE**—an individual's word to give his/her best effort to work for a common cause and to remain loyal to partners and to the organization as a whole. Individuals further promise to sacrifice, when necessary, and to pursue personal needs that align with what is best for the team as a whole.

Power-performance players are competitive partners who make "promises" to each other based upon clearly defined values, principles, strategies and rewards for meeting or exceeding performance expectations. These drivers of peak performance are the underlying emotional forces that energize and unite individuals in order to produce their desired objectives.

The expected outcome of a power-performance contract is rewarding on three mutually-reinforcing, interdependent levels:

- Financially rewarding
- Career enhancing
- Personally satisfying.

Most of the CONTRACTS to build and manage power-performance teams are readily accepted by management gurus and high-potential workers who have their sights set on the executive brass-ring. Others may be considered outside the boundaries of traditional business thinking and practices. A few *contracts* may initially seem paradoxical in that they state behaviors that, on the surface, appear contradictory. Others may even appear to be counter-intuitive and thus be challenged by business professionals who share different experiences and perspectives.

While the 10 Leadership Contracts may occasionally appear philosophical and motivational, they will not be fully effective unless translated into practical action-steps that positively impact an organization's fiscal bottom line and satisfy each partner's personal and professional objectives.

One caution. It is important not to assume that the "contracts" are exclusively material agreements, such as how much money one is paid to do a job. There are important concrete elements that form business partnerships—for example, salary, commission schedules and opportunities for advancement that employees negotiate for the work they produce, as well as, performance expectations that managers hold people accountable for.

The 10 Leadership Contracts go beyond these material agreements. As significant, and at times even more important, there are "psychological contracts" that form an unwritten and occasionally unconscious bond between employers and employees. A *psychological contract* establishes a relationship based on specifically stated or implied behavioral expectations between workers and the powers to be. Trust, respect and loyalty are the underlying forces that forge a relationship that supersede any formal agreement.

Embedded in the **10 Leadership Contracts to Build Power Teams** are the core values that will impact both the people and the fiscal bottom line.

1ST
CONTRACT

COMPETITIVE PARTNERS
PUT AN "I"
IN THE WORD
TEAM

In my opinion, the common belief – *There is no 'I' in the word 'TEAM,'*—is not true. *Power* teams forge a competitive partnership by clearly defining both the personal and professional needs and aspirations of each and every individual ("I need, I expect, I feel, I think, I believe, I appreciate, I will...") and the vision, mission, strategy and values of leaders who are entrusted with the fiduciary responsibilities of the organization.

Many organizations dictate and control the working life of their employees—what, when and how to do things. There is an underlying stated or implied premise that *"I own you between the hours of eight and five."* Although most managers who operate within this outdated structure would not admit it, the underlying reality is *"It's my way or the highway."*

In organizations that promote this type of thinking, the two forces depicted in Figure 2 oppose each other:

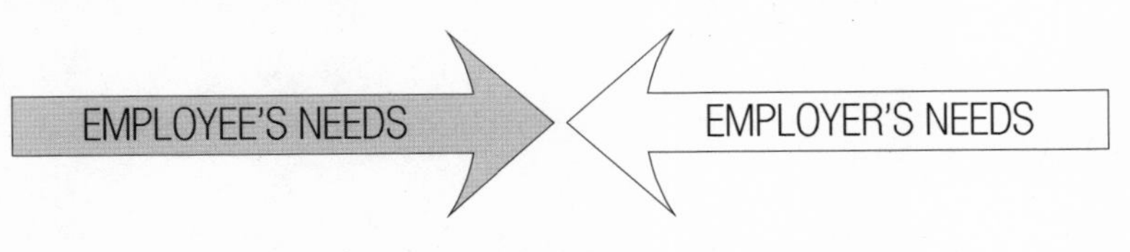

Figure 2.

Managers are not particularly concerned about what an individual thinks or feels, merely whether an employee satisfactorily completes an assigned task. This model acts as if people exist in a bubble—work is on one side of a corporate time-clock and life is on the other side. More progressive organizations realize that employees perform better when they feel valued and when their individual career goals are aligned with the mission of the organization. When managers do their best to promote a more collegial attitude by building personal recognition and material rewards for effort, loyalty and achievement, employees then have the incentives for performing beyond benchmark standards.

In this arrangement, as long as an individual's actions do not conflict with his/her job performance, the boss will encourage the employee's self-improvement efforts and attempts to achieve greater job satisfaction (Figure 3). For example, if a woman hopes to better herself by taking evening classes at a local college, management is supportive, perhaps allowing the employee to leave work early on certain occasions or offering a tuition reimbursement package.

Figure 3.

Permission is typically given with the expectation that one's on-site work will not suffer. If performance declines, managers have the prerogative to remove privileges.

The value of long-term thinking is apparent here—the employee will become more valuable if better educated, not to mention, more satisfied and motivated by a sense of achievement and opportunities that additional professional credentials can bring. The individual is typically further motivated by a belief that managers care about her. All in all, the employee's career path is in sync with the company's objectives.

Power-organizations go even further by making every effort to create a true partnership (Figure 4, next page). This mutually-satisfying alliance between employee and employer not only produces passion and team spirit, it is also just plain smart business—positive, concrete, bottom-line results as a product of the goodwill produced by the spirit of partnership.

This strategy may sound like a win-win scenario. It is more—it is a "win-twice" alliance. *Win-twice* describes a positive, upward spiral that occurs when two forces synergize each other, such as when work-related success and satisfaction produce a greater passion for life, and life-forces, in turn, create energy and excitement to excel at work.

Imagine that there is a competitive partnership between employer and employee, a relationship that challenges an individual to prosper personally and professionally. The employee then takes this passion and goodwill home, feeling successful and rewarded for his/her hard work and dedication. Life at home is also improved, the resulting emotions which, in turn, are brought back to work in the form of loyalty and motivation to raise the bar. In general, this person is loving life!

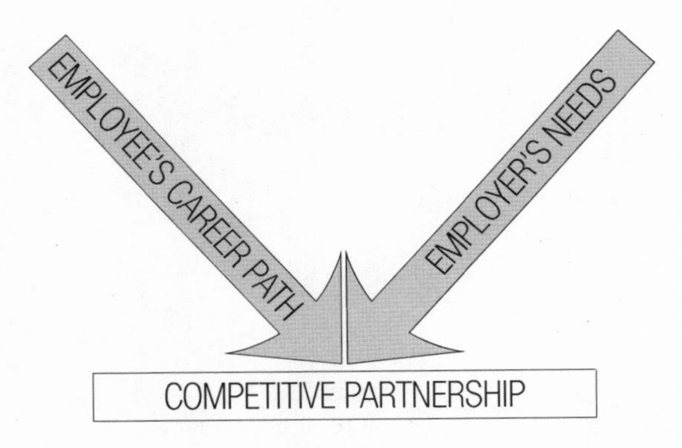

Figure 4.

Dr. John Nash, a Nobel laureate in Economics, summarized this *"win-twice"* concept when he said,

> *"The best result comes when everyone does what is best for him/herself* AND *for the group."*

The old saying,
"Time is money,"
is only partially true.

Building passionate, competitive relationships with motivated partners also enriches everyone involved!

2ND
CONTRACT

BE ACCOUNTABLE TO SELF AND PARTNERS

Members of a *power-team* (*PT*) are driven by pride, passion and a spirit for winning. Second best is never an option. This is in stark contrast to employees who operate under a cloud of fear, compliance and an unhealthy need to please others. The latter traits act as a major distraction absorbing valuable energy from self and others that could be better utilized by focusing attention on actions that hit the primary target—satisfying the needs of the customer.

While financial rewards are important to members of a power-performance team, they are NOT the primary motivation. Wealth, career advancement and other tangible rewards are the results of a person's effort and dedication, NOT the main driving force behind their efforts to succeed. Employees want to feel included in the workings of the operation, as well as, appreciated and recognized for their dedication and sacrifice.

Members of a *P-T* are self-motivated and require low maintenance in relation to managerial supervision. Performance is determined by self-reflection, peer-coaching and behavior modeling, NOT by an unhealthy need for compliance, fear of punishment or anticipated pressure from a superior.

Power performers recognize the fact that this is

My Team
My Career
My Mission
My Company
MY LIFE!

This spirit of ownership empowers behavior based primarily on personal responsibility and reciprocal accountability, not traditional supervision in which a boss has the hierarchical responsibility to keep a close eye on employee performance using both a carrot and a stick—reward for compliance and punishment for non-compliance.

A champion measures success both
by looking into a mirror with the pride of knowing,
"I gave it my best,"

AND

by earning the respect of men and women
who demonstrate the same behavior!

3RD
CONTRACT

THE
TEAM RULE
RULES

Competitive partnerships produce "healthy tension" that require a higher degree of trust—*vulnerability-based trust. Power-teams* need clear, consistent rules of engagement in order to manage conflict in a spirit of *care-frontation,* not destructive confrontation.

Mutual trust and respect evolve in a nurturing environment in which partners feel a responsibility to share experiences and emotions that would—if left unexpressed—cause tension and resistance that negatively impact both the fiscal bottom line and the retention and satisfaction of high performance employees who align with the culture.

The third contract is so powerful, and creates such impact—positive when used correctly versus negative when misused or avoided—perhaps it should be the first contract (it's original name was the "*One Rule*"). I refer to this essential rule of constructive communication as the "Team Rule."

This concept is deceptively simple. It is so easily misunderstood that it is often misused. Let's look at the precise wording of this principle.

"Every individual, regardless of rank or position, is obligated to tell others how they impact him or her —positively and negatively. This information will be in a caring spirit and received as a sign of respect."

You may note that there are three essential parts to the *"Team Rule"*. If a person does not include all three parts in an interpersonal alliance, he/she breaks the third contract.

1)**Every person**, regardless of rank or position, is **obligated** to tell others how they impact him or her—positively and negatively.

The *Team Rule* sets a very high standard of behavior. This is not a mandate for management alone, or any one level. It is for everyone on a team. Also notice the word "obligated." This is intentionally very strong. Individuals have no choice but to do so, if they consider themselves honest and responsible members of a team.

The point is: People who observe something that a partner does— something that impacts how they feel about the partner or perceive him/her to be, personally or professionally—must share that information.

A partner—as a leader, manager, worker, friend, parent or spouse—cannot develop without that knowledge. How can he/she mature as an individual with value and integrity unless he/she knows what co-workers know? How a partner impacts others is of critical importance—both to his/her reputation and future performance. As such, it belongs to him/her.

2) This information—both "facts" and feelings, when considered important for personal and professional development—will be shared in a **caring spirit.**

Notice the emphasis—"in a caring spirit." Partners do not beat each other up. This is not fault-finding, nor abusive confrontation. This is *care-frontation.* Aren't *we* a team? Don't *we* have each other's best interest in mind? If *I* lose, don't *you* lose? And if *I* win, don't *you* win? In this way, don't *you* care?

3) This information will be received as a **sign of respect.**

If partners do their best to show a caring spirit, the information or feedback they provide will be received as a sign of "respect." It will not be seen either as flattery or as criticism. It will be useful to the person receiving it.

Consider this: What is the difference between an individual's reputation and his/her wallet? Again, if partners observe something a person does that significantly weakens his/her leadership position, or something that impacts how others feel about that individual, personally or professionally, aren't they obligated to share that information with their partner? How can a member of a team mature and act in a responsible manner unless he/she knows what their partners know? If a blind person was attempting to cross a busy street, wouldn't people help that person in order to avoid the unseen?

In a similar matter, executives are often *blind* to the impact of their attitudes and behavior — positive and negative. Whose information is it anyway? If people are honest and found someone's wallet, wouldn't they return it to the rightful owner? So, why aren't members of a team expected to give a partner the information that belongs to him/her? Why aren't they as responsible with an individual's reputation?

Oh, by the way, as a leader or business partner, IF *I* DON'T WIN, *YOU* DON'T WIN. Think of the *"win-twice"* possibilities created by constructive feedback. If a partner is not operating up to his/her full potential because of a blind-spot, the team as a whole is diminished!

Take Notice of the Good

One final note regarding the third contract: The *Team Rule* has more to do with what people are doing right than what they are doing wrong. Many leaders neglect a powerful tool that they possess: reinforcing positive behavior. There is a key principle that highlights the value of positive reinforcement: *"People repeat behaviors that pay off."* Why not encourage them to repeat the good by recognizing it? One of the best rewards for employees is recognition. People thirst for recognition and prosper when they are noticed for their best effort.

Wait, There's More

In an earlier publication, "Managers Must Lead and Leaders Must Manage," I discuss a number of business "rules" that I believe significantly impact the performance of executives—what I refer to as *E-Rules,* as in "Executive Rules."

The "E-Rule of Constructive Feedback"

There is a natural phenomenon that occurs as individuals climb the management ladder. Because their "*Psychological Size*" rises, employees stop giving executives constructive feedback—information that is essential if they are to understand and manage the impact that they create by making good and bad decisions.

Psychological Size refers to the perception of importance or value that employees attribute to their bosses because of either a fear how a boss can harm them or because of sheer respect and desire to please and impress a superior.

Psychological size rises to a point that it takes employees into a "No Feedback Zone," a point at which many employees rarely give superiors feedback regarding their behavior. Many even hesitate to express disagreement with a boss regarding issues related to business decisions, sometimes very bad decisions.

Figure 5 illustrates the pattern of behavior that typically occurs as executives climb the career ladder.

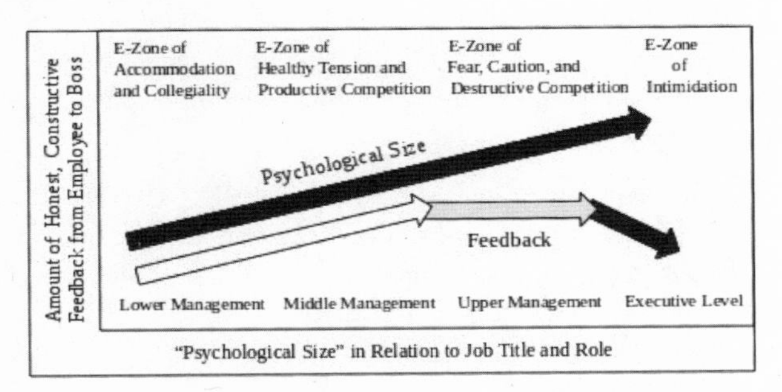

Figure 5.

Figure 5.

As businessmen and -women progress in their careers, honest, constructive feedback rises to a point after which people begin to hold back on information that can impact the bottom line. Things begin to change as managers reach the more senior ranks, a time when people often become more cautious and less collegial, and there is more of a feeling of negative competition and exclusion versus the more positive tone at earlier times in the business relationship.

At the highest ranks, partners enter what I describe as the "E-Zone of Intimidation," where honest and constructive feedback is nearly non-existent. Who wants to give the boss bad news? Employees fear that there will be recrimination if constructive feedback is offered.

It is imperative that executives make it very clear by their words and actions that feedback is a gift, be it positive or negative. On a power-performance team, the TEAM RULE rules!

> "Every person is obligated to tell others
> how they impact him or her—positively and negatively.
> This information will be shared in a caring spirit
> and received as a sign of respect."

4TH
CONTRACT

GOOD INTENTIONS AND BEST EFFORT MAY GET YOU INTO HEAVEN, BUT RESULTS DETERMINE THE GOLD

A person's good intention and best effort are important variables in determining success. When people are highly motivated and passionately engaged in an event they are more likely to produce extra-ordinary results and bring home the "gold medal"—be it in the form of world record competitive performances or business profitability.

But there is more. Ongoing power performances also require that people are "*learning agile,*" which means that they are willing to experience new ways—cognitively and behaviorally—to approach both familiar and unfamiliar situations. Learning agile individuals are open-minded and eager to correct behaviors that produce "performance drag."

Individuals accelerate their growth and improve team performance when they seek and utilize outside feedback. Self-improvement is not solely a "self" process. People do not know what they do not know. Nor do they have "360 degree" perspective. The greatest gift that partners can give each other is constructive feedback—to act as "eyes and ears" for what they are not cognizant of.

If a team is to excel, partners do not settle for the ordinary—they heed the advice of James Collins and strive to go from *"Good to Great."* Not with an unforgiving sense of perfectionism that minimizes best effort in a demoralizing spirit of, *"It's never good enough."* But instead, with a commitment to raise the performance-bar by continuously stretching each individual's personal limits.

A rewarding formula for power performance presented below (Figure 6) states that extra-ordinary business results occur when passionate, dedicated, learning agile partners build a feedback-rich environment. Recognition and reward are provided when one is successful, while constructive criticism is respectfully offered when mistakes can be corrected and improvements are possible.

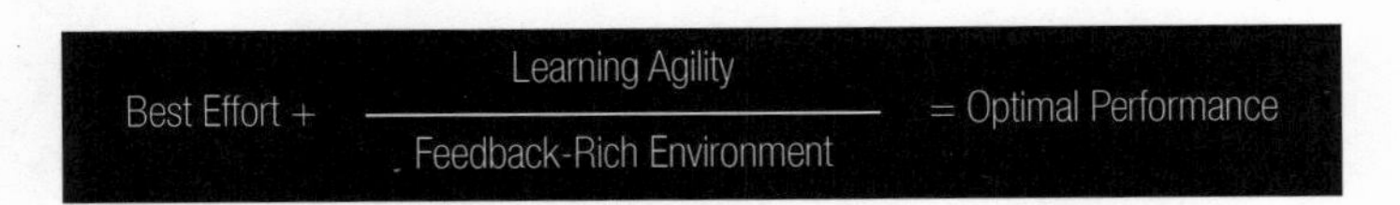

Figure 6.

Learning agility—the willingness to learn from both successes and failures—is a vital ingredient for success. Members of power performance teams are works in progress, never settling on yesterday's output. An open mind is important when things are good, but could be better.

In an effort to build and manage power performance teams, whenever reasonable and appropriate, it is recommended that executives use what is refer to as the "*RECOGNITION-REWARD STRATEGY*," which states:

Leaders publicly and privately RECOGNIZE individuals for best effort, but
REWARD only those who meet or exceed performance expectations.

NOT EVERYONE AGREES

Some executives refuse to utilize the *Recognition-Reward Strategy* by withholding praise if a job is not done correctly. They conclude that expressing appreciation for hard work in the absence of success will signal that it is okay to fail to meet business objectives. The underlying fear is that underachievers, and others who might model their behavior, will assume that recognition in the absence of achievement builds a sense of entitlement and negatively impacts profitability by eroding work ethic.

This concern is understandable. It is generally true—employees should not be *rewarded* for falling short of agreed upon performance standards, even if they work hard. Best effort may get people into heaven, but it could also put a company out of business if that effort and dedication do not produce results. Therefore, **"Outcome is the standard for reward, not effort."**

"Those Who WON'T Are No Better Than Those Who CAN'T!"

Former Baltimore Ravens Head Coach Brian Billick had this stark reminder hanging over his desk during the team's difficult drive to cap off the 2000 season with a victory in Super Bowl XXXV. Having had the privilege to work with Coach Billick, it was clear to me that this message did not lack a spirit of support or caring for his partners. It was the opposite: he expected the best from every one of his players and coaches. Brian set performance-standards as a challenge to **both** those who struggled with personal drive and motivation, as well as, those who needed to raise their skill-sets. After that, he did everything within his power to help individuals to achieve their personal best and recognized their progress, big and small.

Leaders of *power-teams* avoid the trap of "either-or thinking"—people *either* successfully complete a task *or* they receive no recognition for their hard work. Instead they utilize the power of both employee development opportunities: best effort AND task excellence. As the *Recognition-Reward Strategy* urges: *effective leaders publicly and privately recognize employees for best effort, but only reward those who meet or exceed performance expectations.*

The "A-B-C's" of Change

When a person's best effort is present, but the outcome of his/her labor falls short of the agreed upon performance expectation, research demonstrates there are three fundamental components to help change behavior and subsequently improve performance—the "A-B-C's" of change.

The "A"—**A**ntecedents—are what executives do prior to an event to help improve employee performance. Offering encouragement, concrete suggestions and competency-based training are pre-event coaching strategies. Employees also perform better when they are given a preview of an upcoming event. *Visualization*— the ability to use one's imagination as a "feedforward"* technique that mentally previews an upcoming event—is another example of antecedent coaching, similar to how a flight simulator prepares pilots for real-time catastrophic meltdowns.

The letter "B" in a change-management strategy represents the impact that actual behavior has on one's growth and development. People learn by doing. However, experience without positive and negative feedback are missed development opportunities. Experience, combined with constructive, precision-feedback, will accelerate the learning process.

The letter "C" denotes the impact that consequences have on shaping new attitudes and behavior. The research is quite convincing: while all three components are valuable in developing new behavior and improving old habits, the most effective predictor for changes in behavior is the last, viz., consequences. A fundamental performance rule in psychology states:

People repeat behaviors that pay off
and cease doing things that do not pay off.

Recognition and reward for success, as well as, holding people accountable for failing to meet objectives are effective strategies to build performance contracts. A lack of feedback is a missed opportunity to improve partners' behaviors. Praising people for their hard work also positively impacts future

* Feedforward is similar to receiving feedback, except that it is given PRIOR to an event—a form of mental rehearsal.

behavior. Withholding recognition for working hard can dampen employees' spirits by signaling that their best effort is not appreciated.

A lack of feedback may also lower a person's self-esteem and thus negatively impact his/her performance. Failure in the eyes of one's partners can be very painful to the ego—a person often converts the silence of partners into guilt feelings, which undermines confidence and dampens enthusiasm. These emotions can subsequently negatively impact future performances. In the opposite vain, recognizing best effort signals that hard work and dedication are appreciated and stimulates the natural drive in people to do better. People repeat behaviors that pay off—recognition for best effort is a powerful motivating force that drives people to succeed.

As noted, executives often agree with the underlying rationale of the power performance formula, but raise a flag of concern that the Recognition-Reward Strategy could be interpreted as not holding people accountable. That might be true if managers simply praise partners for their hard work but do not take the opportunity—and partnership responsibility—to offer constructive suggestions to improve performance.

In the *"A-B-C's of change,"* consequences for employee behavior are very powerful determinants of future behavior. Executives may send confusing signals when they *reward* people for actions that do not fulfill the agreed upon performance expectations. In the spirit of the "Team Rule" (see 3rd Contract, page 15-16), partners *care-front* one another and create a feedback-rich environment in the hopes of serving each other's desire to succeed.

The research is clear: managers positively impact employees' attitudes and behavior when they praise them for their hard work and dedication. At the same time, the wrong message could be sent if people are given material rewards that have been negotiated in a goal-setting discussion prior to the successful completion of the task. For these reasons, we urge executives to

Celebrate Best Effort
But
Do Not Reward Mediocrity

Positive emotional states create positive emotional consequences for self and others.

Negative emotional states create negative emotional consequences for self and others.

5TH
CONTRACT

PARTNERS ARE YOUR COMPETITION AND YOUR RESPONSIBILITY

The success or failure of one partner impacts every other individual, as well as, the team as a whole. A team is only as strong as its weakest link and as successful as its least successful partner. Destructive competition can result when independent, entrepreneurial behavior is not balanced with a drive to serve partners in their effort to reach their full potential. Effective executives establish systems within the organization that require inter-dependence WITHOUT dampening the independent spirit of high achievers.

Unhealthy competition is counter-productive to the success of an organization and typically kills team spirit. Guidelines for inter-dependence are as follows:

- ✓ I win-you win and vice versa—when you win-I win.
- ✓ I lose-you lose and vice versa—when you lose-I lose.
- ✓ Partners do their best to help others to succeed.
- ✓ Partners know that the more one person succeeds, the more we all succeed.
- ✓ Partners feel good about accomplishments of others and of the organization.
- ✓ Partners share information generously.
- ✓ Partners sacrifice their own good for the good of the team.
- ✓ Partners collaboratively solve problems.
- ✓ There is a full personal commitment to the big picture.
- ✓ Each individual does more than his/her own share when needed, gladly.
- ✓ Partners address conflict and catch others doing the right thing.
- ✓ Peer-coaching benchmarks standards and optimizes performance.
- ✓ Partners provide support and encouragement to each other. When they cannot add direct value to the efforts of others, they find opportunities to recognize people's best effort and cheer them on.

Successful teams build inter-dependent systems around highly independent people.

AND
they compensate people
based on each individual's level of success—
the more you achieve, the more you are rewarded.

6TH
CONTRACT

WHEN IT COMES TO JOB ROLE...

MAY THE FORCE BE WITH YOU

Business success, across industries, is the result of interaction and ongoing reinforcing synergy between three primary forces—Three Core Competencies:

1. Business Fundamentals **(F)**
2. Interpersonal skills **(Ip)**
3. Authentic Self **(S)**

BUSINESS FUNDAMENTALS (F)—Knowledge, skill, ability, and experience are essential in order to provide the expertise necessary to accomplish the strategic objectives of any organization. Business fundamentals are the foundation of a successful performance, whether it is selling wallpaper in Paducah or competing for the starting quarterback position on the Baltimore Ravens football team. Every job—from the copy room to the boardroom—requires fundamental core competencies.

INTERPERSONAL SKILLS (Ip)—Business is conducted between people. Therefore, **I**nter**p**ersonal Skills (Ip) are important success ingredients. Employees do not operate in a business vacuum and generally must have regular contact with partners throughout the organization. Interpersonal skills allow people to communicate effectively and build mutual understanding about what is expected from the relationship they share—who does what, when, where, how and why. When associates constructively interact, an affiliation is established ranging from a formal, superficial, impersonal and primarily business-based connection to a more personal, collegial and even friendship-based interaction.

SELF—Because individuals have personal motives beyond career objectives and project a particular image to others, **S**elf forces impact the outcome of events. The degree of passion one brings to an event and the impressions created by that individual, generate either favorable or unfavorable responses from co-workers, which in turn affect each other's thoughts, feelings and behaviors. Furthermore, how an individual feels about himself will also significantly impact his behavior. Self-esteem and self-confidence—be they high versus low—will help determine whether an individual succeeds or fails at tasks that are well within his/her range of opportunity.

Henry Ford defined the power of "self forces" when he said,

"Whether you believe you can or believe you can't,
you're always right."

***

The Matrix of Three Primary Forces Determine Roles

Roles within teams—Expert, Manager, Leader—arise according to the sequence of core competencies (see Figure 7):

Perceived/Intended Role on POWER Performance Teams	Primary Force	Vehicle	Background
EXPERT →	F	Ip	S
MANAGER →	Ip	F	S
LEADER →	S	Ip	(F)

Figure 7

EXPERT—The primary goal of operations-level employees is to become highly proficient in a particular subject matter, i.e., gain a high-degree of expertise in a particular topic or task. Experts are the *worker-bees* who are invested in pure performance. They deliver what managers define as the practical, operational efforts to reflect the organizational values and accomplish a mission in a timely manner.

Experts are also expected to share specific information and support those who are attempting to understand or utilize such expertise through the "vehicle" of interpersonal interaction (Ip). If someone is smart and proficient, but is misunderstood, unavailable, or not perceived as approachable, then his/her contributions will be minimized.

MANAGERS have a dual **Ip** focus: to establish interpersonal relationships and effectively communicate with their direct reports. Managers are also institutional bridges between senior leaders and employees—explaining and promoting the vision, mission and strategic objectives, as well as, assigning tasks, monitoring performance and holding people accountable for the final outcome.

While trusting, partner-relationships are always important to build and unite teams, the primary focus of the manager is to hold each direct report accountable in relation to performance expectations. Did s/he meet or exceed the negotiated goals?

Managers deliver a vision through four practical "P's":

1. PURPOSE—Why are we moving in a particular direction?
2. PICTURE—What will it look like when we reach our goal?

3. PLAN—How will we get there?

4. PERSONAL—What can I (must I) do to help us succeed?

LEADERSHIP—In the role of a LEADER, the primary goal is to proactively reflect a robust, capable, passionate *Authentic Self* (**S**). Leaders express and model the core values and cultural norms that drive them. As the saying goes:

"Actions speak louder than words."

Leaders are a living reflection of their values and vision. Success in a leadership role is measured by the degree to which followers identify with, adopt, and act upon their leaders' visions and values. **The message and the messenger become one.** One final comment regarding Figure 7. Note that the **"F"**—denoting a leader's level of fundamental expertise—is in parenthesis. A leader is not necessarily the greatest subject matter expert on a team. Leaders must recognize talent and surround themselves with competent partners. But their job has more to do with inspiration than perspiration, creating passion and vision rather than hands on delivery of services.

As former President Ronald Reagan said,

"A leader is not necessarily
the one who does great things.
A great leader is one who gets people to do great things."

ONE TEAM... Partners United in a Common Cause

Like a three-legged stool, each role is important in order to support the institutional mission. Remove or diminish one role and the stool will topple.

Success is a team effort. No one group—expert, manager or leader—is more important than the other. Leaders and managers share a special reciprocal relationship, each doing some of what the other does. While there are similarities and shared services, there are also distinct differences which are described in detail in an earlier publication:

"Managers Must Lead—Leaders Must Manage."

While success is a team effort, leadership is not! Leadership in and of itself is a solitary process related to the **S**elf. A common misconception of executive development is that one simply continues along the career path from expert to manager and eventually to a leadership role by adding "psychological size," rank, and business skills to his/her portfolio. It is important NOT to confuse power and authority with leadership. Just because someone outranks direct reports does not mean s/he is an effective leader. Leadership is not defined by rank alone.

Research by Korn Ferry, an international consulting group, has validated these impressions and reinforced the importance of self-development as a primary ingredient to successfully climb the executive career ladder. Ambitious employees asked the question, *"What will help support my efforts to enter the leadership pipeline in my organization?"*

Researchers noted that there are four primary components:

1. **Effort and Expertise (F)**... Build credibility and respect through work-ethic and skill-building that meet or exceed benchmark standards. Execute tasks for on-time delivery.

2. **Strategic Thinking (F)**... Work smart by aligning business strategy with customer needs and market opportunities.

3. **Diverse Teams (Ip)**... Build strong bonds and dedicated commitments between individuals of various races, genders, religions, life-experiences, academic backgrounds, and business perspectives.

4. **Self (S)**... Build passionate partnerships based upon both character and competency that align with institutional goals and expectations.

In Figure 7A, over twenty-one thousand aspiring executives in top performing organizations across the country were followed for nearly twenty years.

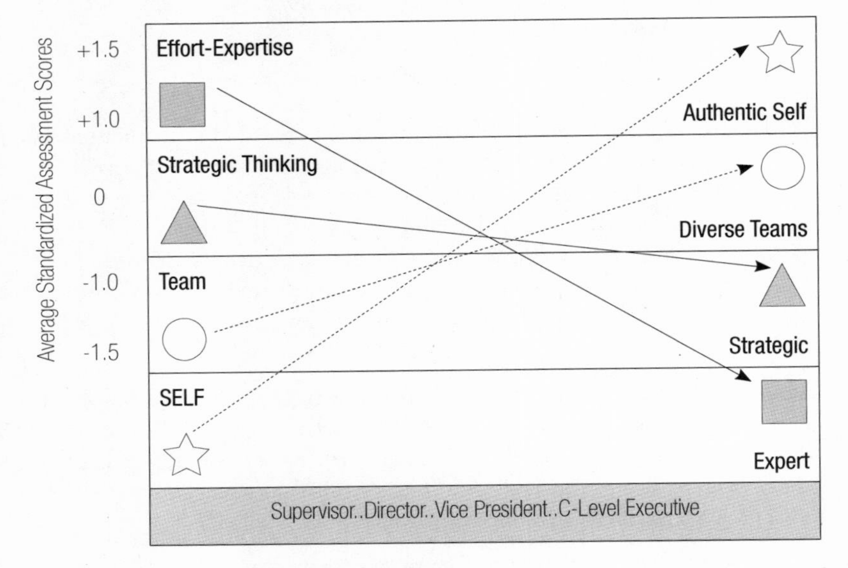

FIGURE 7A

The data is clear: one must work hard (Effort and Expertise) and work smart (Strategic Thinking) in order to be considered for management positions. Team-building skills and self-development, while always important, are weighted less in the initial selection process relative to traditional business fundamentals. BUT, notice what happens as careers advance. Those who succeed in a **leadership role** do so because they shifted their primary focus from expertise (Business Fundamentals and Strategy) to personal authenticity (Self) and passionate partnerships (what we will define in the next *Contract* as "R2 and R3" relationships). The key value and prominence of forces related to the Self become more significant in relation to what people look for in a leader, as well as, the desire to build diverse teams.

This does not in any way diminish the importance of expertise and strategic thinking. But it does illustrate a shift from business X's and O's to Self and person-to-person opportunities. C-Level Executives (C.E.O., C.O.O., C.F.O., etc.) are NOT graded primarily on their expertise. People want to know who their leaders are, as well as, a whole host of character and interpersonal questions, including:

"Can I trust you with my life and my career?"

The Power of "R" (Relationships)

While I was congratulating Jim Fassel for his championship victory as Head Coach of the United Football League *Las Vegas Locomotives,* he reminded me of a quote I had shared when he was facing a challenge while the Offensive Coordinator of the Baltimore Ravens:

"People don't care how much you KNOW
until they know how much you CARE.*"*

The coach went on to say, *"I opened and closed the season with this message. It's my job as a team leader to let players and staff know that our partnership goes beyond the gridiron statistics and the number of wins versus losses. I'm responsible for their well-being, celebrate their best efforts and offer them support, guidance, and a loving kick-in-the-ass when they're not fully focused. It's about caring... really caring!"*

Coach Fassel stands head-to-head with another leader that I admire, John Carey, a man who helped build an exceptional enterprise with his unique vision:

"Strive for Excellence Through Serving Others."

While entrepreneurial geniuses like Bill Gates were building empires upon traditional product and process deliverables, Mr. Carey was in the trenches with his team challenging them to first invest in each other. By helping partners build personal dreams and holding them accountable to achieve their goals, John challenged the dictum: *"There is no "I" in the word 'TEAM'."*

In the spirit of the 1st Contract, he puts an "I" in the word TEAM: a capital "I" when something is non-negotiable, versus a small "i", when someone is willing to sacrifice and thus take one for the team.

Working hard and working smart never become unimportant in the business success equation. But these traits and behaviors alone will not make you an effective leader, nor do they solely determine a *power* performance.

Businesses are filled with experts who are unaware of the evidence in the Korn Ferry research and have not been inspired by leaders like Coach Fassel and John Carey. Peter Drucker sums up the evidence with firm advice:

"The very things that got you to this point in your career may have to be abandoned (or at least refocused) in order to continue along the executive career path!"

Less effective leaders micromanage the hell out of their direct reports, demanding effort and outcome WITHOUT developing trusting relationships and a spirit of ownership based on personal pride, shared values, and a common mission. There is *POWER* in a balance between traditional know-how (IQ) and passionate partner-relationships (EQ)*.

I urge you to consider the advice of Daniel Goleman, author of the book, "*Emotional Intelligence*":

"IQ will get you hired,
but EQ will get you promoted."

Warren Bennis, author of such classics as, *"On Becoming a Leader,"* agrees:

"Research clearly shows that the vast majority of executives who fail in their jobs do so because of behavioral and cultural issues, not because of lack of skill or experience.

It therefore seems odd that most of the emphasis on succession planning, hiring and promoting still focuses largely on evaluating skill and experience."

Manager's Golden Rule

Power performance arises from managing the on-time expression of the fundamental KSA's in an action-environment that recognizes best effort and rewards those who meet performance expectations.

Leadership Golden Rule

No matter where you are
or what you are doing,
first build relationships,
then focus on the task.

* EQ (Emotional Intelligence) is the social, emotional, and self variables that allow individuals to build special personal and professional bonds by sharing the Authentic Self with partners.

7TH
CONTRACT

LEADERSHIP IS A MATTER OF SEIZING OPPORTUNITIES TO ADD VALUE,
NOT TITLE, RANK OR POSITION-POWER

True leadership is not a matter of traditional power and authority derived from title, rank or position. It has more to do with seizing opportunities to add value to business initiatives. A core principle underlying a competitive partnership is a spirit of ownership. No, an individual does not necessarily have to own actual stock in the company—although that would help motivate any peak performer! Partnership is more about feeling valued and having a sense of control of the actual outcome of achieving a goal. Even more important, it is about making one's job a vehicle to building a special life with material rewards, personal satisfaction and social recognition.

In power-organizations, each person is made to feel as if he/she is vital to the success of the mission—there is no such thing as a small job or an insignificant role. If a person does not add value to the success equation, he/she should not be in a job or on a team. In addition, on a power performance team, each person is recognized, respected and made to feel significant. *Bosses* go out of their way to understand what drives their employees. "What is your 'burn,'" is asked—that is, "What motivates you to succeed? What lights a fire in your belly?"

The research is quite clear in regards to what people value. When surveyed, employees report that they desire three things more than anything else, including job security and pay raises:

1. Interesting work

2. Appreciation for work done

3. Being in on things

The recommendation embedded in the 7th Contract is:

IF you have institutional power, share it.

If you lack organizational authority, find opportunities to add value to a business equation. Real power has more to do with contributing to the business strategy and bottom-line profitability than with rank, position, or title.

If you are looking for structure and permission to act in a contributing manner, you are a welcome member of a power-performance team—a good "soldier" ready to carry out an order and add expertise to a mission.

If you want to LEAD, you cannot afford to just sit back and wait to be told what to do. Look, listen and learn. Then act.

Power Must Be Seized,
It cannot Be Given

8TH CONTRACT

POWER-TEAMS MAKE DOLLARS AND CENTS BY MAKING DOLLARS AND SENSE

COMMON SENSE

Peter Drucker, a well-respected business guru who recently passed away at ninety-seven years of age, warns executives that nearly 85 of all strategic change initiatives that have been done correctly, FAIL!

Why? Because they forget to include one very significant factor...the human work force. The power of an organization is in its people. Men and women do not leave their lives and whole-self at the door when they report to work. It's common sense.

Establishing strong inter-personal relationships based on mutual trust and respect are the "main thing" in building highly profitable organizations that are "built to last." Strategy alone will not get it done. There is an *"R-Factor"* that drives world class strategies.

What is the "R-Factor?"

The *R-Factor* has three primary components:

I. Relationships

II. **Relationships**

III. **RELATIONSHIPS**

The bonds between people are like the batteries in the Energizer Bunny. Without an on-going power source, the bunny is an inert object with little working value. Relationships generally lie on three primary levels depending on the degree of closeness and level of risk people are willing to take to form person-to-person bonds. Each level has a unique power source that unites individuals. The lower the level, the less committed and driven people tend to be toward achieving a common cause.

Leaders of Power-Teams
Expect Level II Relationships
AND
Strive for Level III Relationships

Level I—Relationships are casual, relatively guarded, cryptic, closed or private. Individuals may be willing to share some selective personal information **IF** asked.

Level II—Relationships are more proactively open. Partners take the initiative to share their true "story"—significant events that have impacted them and made them the people they are today. There is a higher level of mutual trust in which individuals tend to build a bond that goes beyond ordinary working relationships.

Level III—Relationships are more intimate because partners not only share the "what" of their stories, but also the "so what"—emotional impact—and "now what"—lessons-learned and action-alternatives.

Level III relationships contain at least four things:

1. Vulnerability based trust—partners share important life information that illustrate sensitivity and offers a more personal window to the self.
2. More open, honest sharing of both positive and negative thoughts and feelings, including a willingness to *care-front* partners in the spirit of the *Team Rule* regarding issues that negatively impact their relationship.
3. Deeper level of respect as a result of sharing significant insights to the self.
4. Unconditional acceptance—a sense of loyalty to protect the good name and best interests of partners.

For those who hope to lead a power-performance team, let me repeat the "Leadership Golden Rule"—

> *No matter where are. No matter what you are doing.*
> *First build relationships, then, focus on tasks and execution.*

In my opinion, it's common sense, not rocket science. The research and experience reinforce this perspective. For example, Daniel Golemen, author of "**Emotional Intelligence**," insists,

> *"The rules for work are changing. We're being judged by a new yardstick: Not just how smart we are, or our expertise, but also how well we handle ourselves and each other."*

Most strategic change initiatives fizzle and crash because of a lack of buy-in on the grassroots level. Executives often invest in big ideas, but neglect to truly involve the people who actually drive the initiative. It's like buying an expensive, sophisticated toy without including the batteries to animate it.

AN EXECUTIVE DILEMMA

Upwardly mobile men and women strive to climb the career ladder. It takes most executives time to realize that rank truly has privileges. However, a powerful paradox also evolves. Rank supposes power. This is both true and false.

There is a false belief that an executive's ability to control his/her destiny increases the higher he/she rises on the corporate leadership ladder. One of the many paradoxes that executives face is that, on the one hand, rank and seniority offer enormous opportunity to present a vision for others to act upon. On the other hand, there is little, if any, direct power in leadership itself.

Executives generally do not deliver a primary product, employees do that. In sales organizations for example, it is the line-level salesperson who breaks an account and services clients, not a leader. In education, it is the classroom teacher, not the principal or superintendent, who impacts the academic "bottom line"—that is, actually helps children on a daily basis to grow intellectually, emotionally and socially. And finally in a military battle, the generals do not bring down the enemy. That is the job of the soldiers on the front line.

In each example—business, education, military—success is not primarily in the hands of a leader or manager. It is the result of vision combined with a concrete strategy and action-plan. However, without action, vision is little more than daydreaming.

THE POWER GRADIENT PRINCIPLE

According to Dr. Ichak Adizes in his book, "Managing Corporate Lifecycles," there are three primary executive options:

1. **POWER** (as traditionally defined): The capacity to reward and penalize employees.
2. **AUTHORITY**: The right to make a decision—to say "yes" or "no" to change.
3. **INFLUENCE**: The capacity to cause employees to act without having to invoke power or authority.

We propose the **"Power Gradient Principle"** as a methodology to produce power-performance behavior:

"While executives have the right to use power and authority, except under special circumstances, dynamic leaders use influence with their direct reports, and place power and authority in the hands of employees lower in the chain-of-command, closer to the point of customer service."

World-class vision and strategy can fail when executives ignore common sense, namely, placing power and authority where it belongs—in the hands of those who need it in order to drive a mission and deliver customer satisfaction.

PARTNER-RELATIONSHIPS
are the driving forces
that produce

RESULT$

9TH
CONTRACT

PROMOTE THE "3-A RULE"

Talk and planning are good.

Listening is often even better.

What is best?

The bottom line to business success is guided by three A's:

action
Action
ACTION

Enough said.

Power performers do what less successful people say they will do, **BUT DON'T!**

Power Leaders
Turn Belief Into
ACTION

10TH
CONTRACT

LOOK FOR THE HORSE

OPTIMISM —to the surprise of many—is a learned trait. It is a choice that individuals make by either positively responding to challenging situations with a "half-full," self-enhancing perspective, rather than negatively reacting to performance opportunities with a "half-empty," self-defeating mindset. The research by Martin Seligman ("*Learned Optimism*") and others is quite clear, viz., people are not born with either a positive frame-of-mind or naturally burdened as nay-Sayers.

People are born *tabula rosa*—clean slates. Significant historical positive and negative occurrences—"marker events"—shape an individual's general outlook on life.

Assessing one's degree of optimism versus pessimism is not just a way of gauging a person's style of thinking. It is a predictor of concrete behaviors that measure the differences between power performers, who perceive opportunity in the face of conflict as a "can do" event, versus underachievers, who see the same situation than an optimist faces, but interprets it very differently—viz., a "can't do" event.

Businessmen and -women have a competitive advantage when they adopt an optimistic, "can-do" perspective of their world. As noted earlier, Henry Ford put it best when he said,

"If you believe you can or believe you can't,
you're always right."

A reminder to those who are facing adversity,

On your journey through the field of life,
when you step in horse manure,
you can stand there cursing,
OR
YOU CAN LOOK FOR THE HORSE

Where there is horse manure (conflict), there is a horse (opportunity).

A DEFECTIVE COACHING MODEL FOR CHANGE

Most people fail in their attempts to change their negative responses to challenging situations—not because they do not want to alter their behavior, nor because they refuse to work hard on an alternative strategy. The reason they fail is because they are using a defective change-model.

The usual model used to explain how events impact people is as follows:

Figure 8: **Model A:**

According to the above model (Figure 8), an event triggers a person's feelings, which in turn cause him/her to react with a specific set of behaviors. For example, Ted—not his real name—is driving home from work at a moderate rate of highway speed. He's feeling good after a successful day in the office. Out of nowhere, a *road warrior* cuts him off, forcing his way into Ted's driving lane. Instantly, Ted's mood changes.

According to Model A, the event—reckless maneuvering by an aggressive driver—causes Ted to feel angry, which in his case triggers reactive road rage.

If a friend or a manager were coaching Ted, she might urge him to react differently. "Don't let aggressive drivers upset you," she advises. "Instead of letting him get you angry, back off and turn on a favorite radio channel to distract yourself." Thoughtful suggestions. But do they work? Not usually over the long run.

Hot reactions like road rage tend to be deeply engrained and resurface after a close call with the police or the comforting advice of a coach. The reason that negative behavior tends to repeat itself is in the model itself. Model A proposes that an event triggers a person's emotions, which in turn shapes his/her behavior. **NOT TRUE**.

There is an additional step (see Figure 9: Model B) embedded between an event and one's emotional reaction, viz., an individual's **belief** related to the event. A person's belief, perception, and assumptions trigger his/her emotions, not the event itself. An individual's belief acts like a filter, just as eyeglasses alter an image for a person with near- or far-sighted vision.

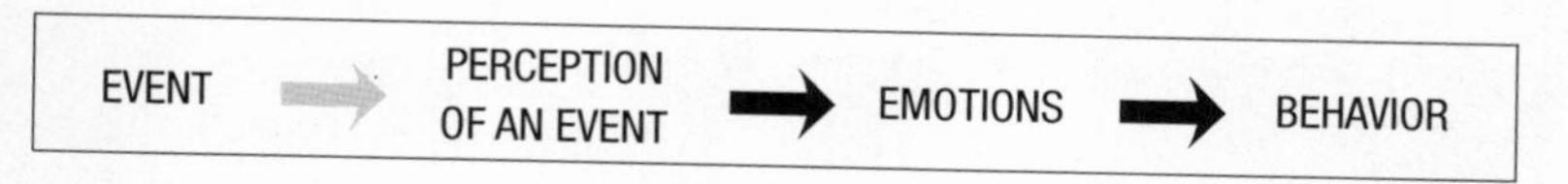

Figure 9: **Model B:**

If people positively change their underlying interpretation of an event, they will alter their emotions, which in turn produces more constructive behavior.

When "Ted" had a brush with the law for reckless endangerment with a motor vehicle, he saw himself as a victim, not a perpetrator. He complained that the police unjustly ticketed him for his reaction. During an executive coaching session he adamantly protested, "I was just minding my business. This idiot cut me off. It was not my fault. He made me angry!"

The short version of this story is that Ted believed that the other driver was trying to take advantage of him— "Who the hell does he think he's pushing around," he said. "Does he think that I'll just roll over like some kind of wimp?" He decided, as usual, to fight back. Ted had the reputation of a "hot reactor"—a man with a short emotional fuse.

These feelings were common for Ted; he was used to feeling pushed around and abused. Ted's life had been filled with a recurring theme from marker events between him and his father—recurring events that shaped his perception of the world. As a child and teenager, his Dad—a good man, who thought he was helping his son—constantly criticized him. Dad thought he was challenging his son to change his self-defeating behavior when he would say, "You're an idiot," whenever Ted made a mistake. Without admitting it to himself, Ted began to feel like a loser.

Ted was polite and patient when we explored his perceptions of the highway incident. I believe that he initially thought my inquiry was little more than psycho-babble. He gradually changed his mind when asked to consider a different scenario:

You're driving home at a safe, reasonable speed, minding your own business. Suddenly, you're ambushed by a reckless driver.

I asked Ted how he felt at this point. He described his anger in rather graphic, street language. Then I added one further piece of information:

This driver is not an aggressive road warrior. He is a frantic father rushing his five-month old child to a hospital emergency room. The baby has a raging fever and is struggling to breathe.

I sensed an immediate change in Ted's emotions. The anger in his face shifted to one of compassion. When asked how he might react in this situation, he quickly responded that he would give way–

"I'd move aside. I only wish that I was a cop so I could part the traffic like Moses parted the Red Sea."

What changed? The event is still the same—an aggressive driver cuts Ted off. Why are his emotions different? Ted has an alternate, less ego-threatening interpretation of the event (Figure 10).

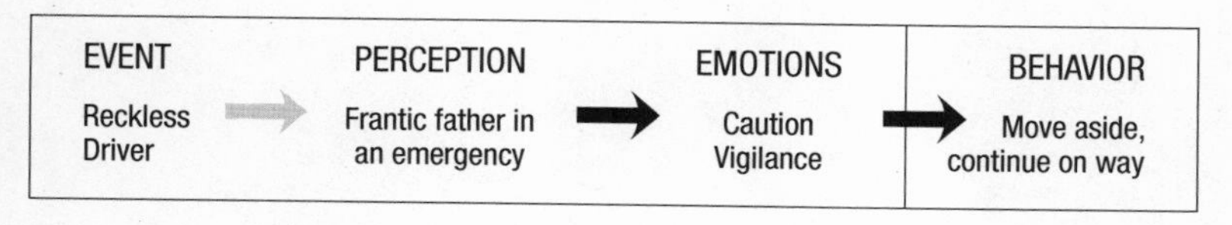

Figure 10.

Whether a person knowingly or unintentionally creates a problem for us, or when we feel overwhelmed by a difficult situation, the effective response is to avoid destructive, self-defeating confrontation. As the old saying goes,

"If you're not part of the solution,
you're part of the problem."

If you must care-front a person, I urge you to use the TEAM RULE—all three critical parts. You're also advised to:

Think positively.

Share your thoughts, feelings, needs and desired outcomes.

Listen for complete understanding of the other person's perspective.

And above all ...

LOOK FOR THE HORSE!

CLOSING THOUGHTS

BUSINESS PARADOX—What is the Secret to Success?

Executives across industries struggle with a business paradox:

Which is more important in relation to the
long-term success of an organization—
business strategy and fundamental job operations
OR
interpersonal relationships?

Is it the constant pressure to impact the business bottom line—driving sales up, while keeping operational costs down—that is the primary marker of success? Or is it the people-side of this paradox—how to motivate and lead the men and women who produce the actions necessary to build and sustain profitability?

I'd like to offer a response to the business paradox—one that is based on nearly forty years of direct professional experience and by a dearth of research. **Rule #1** to clarify this business paradox is:

There Is NO Paradox

This is not a sarcastic or tongue-in-cheek remark. It's a reminder that **people drive businesses** and person-to-person relationships are the reason why individuals work harder than their competition. Unless individuals are highly motivated to succeed, they do not produce extra-ordinary business results.

To athletic superstars who are repeat winners, as well as, corporate champions who establish benchmark standards for success and profitability, *contracts* are what forge individual contributors into *power-teams*. Like individual fingers working together as one hand, when people unite in a common cause, they have the option to act like a fist to apply force when needed and like an open hand when meeting and greeting new partnership opportunities.

Every organization—in business, sports, community and family—benefits when people consistently act with the passion of owners who constantly support, counsel, drive, console and challenge each other. Best practices become the ever-escalating norm of excellence—never accepting what is "the best," because *"best"* is a temporal reality that can change with the next *power* performance.

Contracts—**promises made and promises kept**—are the energy source that build power-performance teams. Contracts are promises to serve one's self, significant others, peer-partners, and the organization as a whole. To do one's best and to expect the same from every passionate, like-minded individual. Partners are united in a common cause by contracts, seeking the rewards, recognition and satisfaction from winning—best effort in mind, body and spirit.

Now It's Your Turn...

The TEN LEADERSHIP CONTRACTS can be your call-to-arms to men and women who are looking for a cause to follow and a leader who will serve them in their career adventures.

I have a final wish for you...

May You Dream, But Not Be a Dreamer

10 LEADERSHIP CONTRACTS

To Build POWER Teams

*

Passion . **O**wnership . **W**ellness . **E**xcellence . **R**elationships

1st	Competitive partners put an "I" in the word "TEAM"
2nd	Be accountable to self and partners
3rd	The *Team Rule* rules
4th	Good intentions and best effort may get you into heaven, but results determine the gold
5th	Partners are your competition AND your responsibility
6th	When it comes to job role... —Expert, Manager, Leader— "May the *force* be with you"
7th	Leadership is a matter of seizing opportunities to add value, NOT title, rank or position-power
8th	*Power-teams* make dollars and *CENTS* by making dollars and *SENSE*—Common Sense
9th	Promote the *"3-A Rule"*
10th	Look for the horse!

SIDEBAR regarding “POWER **Performance**”

There is a long list of words to describe extraordinary levels of success. There are books that explore peak performance, optimal impact, and so on. Stephen Covey uses the term “Highly Effective People” in his book, “The Seven Habits of….”

I refer to: “**POWER**” performance.

To me, the expression is more than a bumper sticker saying on steroids. The term is an acronym used in an attempt to “connect the dots” between key forces to build and maintain exceptional, repeatable performance.

While business fundamentals such as knowledge, skill, ability, and experience are essential ingredients for success, a “power” performance is the result of institutional, interpersonal, cultural, and self-forces.

P.O.W.E.R. performers form partnerships around:

Passion
Ownership
Wellness
Excellence
Relationships

Passionate Commitment…

On a power-team, passion is never an option.
It is an obligation to meet or exceed expectations.

Ownership…

Act as if you have skin in the game.

The spirit of ownership is measured by a belief that this is **my** company, **my** team, **my** life, **my** opportunity to….

It is not necessarily determined by having an actual stake in a venture (although this is an important and valid motivator).

Wellness…

Through life-work balance.

Work is a vehicle to deliver individual dreams that make our one-hundred-year journey through life a satisfying and rewarding experience for ourselves and those significant others who we attempt to serve through hard work and sacrifice. Becoming successful **at the expense of** our health and well-being makes no sense personally or professionally. You are the "goose that lays the golden eggs." If YOU are not well, WE are not well...peak performance is impossible; we as a team are diminished when any individual is operating with any one or more of the *POWER* forces missing or minimized.

Excellence...

Extraordinary outcome.

Power players operate within a performance culture. Results matter! While best effort is always recognized and celebrated, the reward goes to the winners... those who meet and exceed benchmark standards!

Relationships...

Bonds grounded in shared values, goals and expectations.

Partners celebrate best efforts **and** care enough to hold one another accountable for their performance and the impact each creates. P-O-W-E-R performers add an "**R**-Factor" to the traditional success formula: work hard, work smart, **and** build passionate partner-relationships based on mutual trust and respect.

Last, but not least, power performers create healthy tension by building contracts based on the principle:

"My partners are my competition and my responsibility."

ABOUT THE AUTHOR

Joseph R. Currier, Ph.D., is a licensed psychologist and management consultant, who has devoted his career to helping people change the self-defeating attitudes and break through barriers of resistance that prevent them from leading healthier, happier, and more productive lives.

In his years of professional dedication, Dr. Currier has been involved in leadership development, executive coaching, succession planning, change-transition management, crisis intervention and team building with a wide variety of organizations such as The Allegis Group, Baltimore Ravens NFL Franchise, Mobil Oil, KPMG, Wachovia Bank and the United States Forest Service. He frequently serves as a personal coach and consultant to senior executives, professional athletes and team coaches.

Dr. Currier is the Chief Learning Officer for The Allegis Group, helping to establish a corporate university and directing its Executive Institute. Joe has been a senior psychological associate with four of the premier outplacement companies: Jannotta Bray, Right Associates, Lee Hecht Harrison and Drake Beam Morin. He is a faculty member of the Bernard H. Ehrlich Executive Management Institute (EMI) at the University of Maryland, and a former professor and graduate department chairperson at Hofstra University.

Dr. Currier is the author of the book-audio series, *"Leadership Is Always Simple But Never Easy."* His innovative work to foster personal and professional growth include workshops like: *"The Art of Leadership", "Lead . Follow . OR Hide", and "Survive OR Prosper."*

Joe also wrote and narrated two other audio series: *"How to Manage Stress"* and *"Less Stress,"* as well as, authored, *"Connect the Dots—How Significant Life Events Impact Your Life, Leadership Style and Competitive Performance," "Managers Must Lead and Leaders Must Manage", and "If You're So Damn Smart, Why Aren't You Healthier and More Effective?"*

To learn more about Dr. Joe Currier and his work with the Currier Consulting Group, Inc., you can visit his website:

www.currierconsultinggroup.com

Or contact him at: Joe@currierconsultinggroup.com

Printed in Canada